Dedicated to all the children who live in the Canadian Boreal Forest, especially those who acted as my consultants for this book. I hope this answers most of your questions about the porcupine.

The author gratefully acknowledges the insightful comments and information provided by Thomas Jung, Senior Biologist, Department of Environment, Yukon.

Also by Olga Majola

I Am A Fox Let Me Tell You About Myself
I Am A Moose Let Me Tell You About Myself

Olga Majola
Northern Forest Animal Books
3130 Louise St. Apt. 101
Saskatoon, SK S7J 3L8
omajola2002@yahoo.ca

Note for Librarians: A cataloguing record for this book is available from Library and Archives Canada at www.collectionscanada.ca/amicus/index-e.html
ISBN 1-4120-9563-8

Printed in Victoria, BC, Canada. Printed on paper with minimum 30% recycled fibre. Trafford's print shop runs on "green energy" from solar, wind and other environmentally-friendly power sources.

TRAFFORD
PUBLISHING™
Offices in Canada, USA, Ireland and UK

This book was published *on-demand* in cooperation with Trafford Publishing. On-demand publishing is a unique process and service of making a book available for retail sale to the public taking advantage of on-demand manufacturing and Internet marketing. On-demand publishing includes promotions, retail sales, manufacturing, order fulfilment, accounting and collecting royalties on behalf of the author.

Book sales for North America and international:
Trafford Publishing, 6E–2333 Government St.,
Victoria, BC V8T 4P4 CANADA
phone 250 383 6864 (toll-free 1 888 232 4444)
fax 250 383 6804; email to orders@trafford.com
Book sales in Europe:
Trafford Publishing (UK) Limited, 9 Park End Street, 2nd Floor
Oxford, UK OX1 1HH UNITED KINGDOM
phone 44 (0)1865 722 113 (local rate 0845 230 9601)
facsimile 44 (0)1865 722 868; info.uk@trafford.com
Order online at:
trafford.com/06-1318

10 9 8 7 6 5 4 3 2

I am a porcupine. I belong to the rodent family.

In Canada, I am the second largest rodent; only the beaver is larger than I am. Like all rodents, I have four large orange front teeth. I am active at night. This makes me a nocturnal animal.

When I am fully-grown I will be 80 – 135 cm (31 – 53 inches) long. This includes my tail, which is between 15-30 cm long (6 – 12 inches). My height will be about 30 cm (12 inches) and I will weigh between 5 and 18 kilograms (11 – 40 pounds).

I was born in June but other porcupettes (baby porcupines) could be born any time between the middle of April and late June. Porcupines almost always give birth to only one baby at a time, so I was the only baby my mother had that year. I have a father but he doesn't live with us.

I am born with my eyes open and I am able to see. I weighed about half a kg (a bit more than one lb.) and I was about 30 cm (12 inches) long.

Within an hour of my birth two wonderful things happened! I could walk and climb by myself; and my quills, which were very soft when I was born, became stiff enough for me to defend myself.

My mother and I continue to nest in an open space between some
rocks. I depend on my mother's milk for about a month. However,
when I am two weeks old I am strong enough to follow my mother
and nibble on twigs, leaves and herbs.

There are so many wonderful things to see around me and under me!
On the ground there are trees, bushes, flowers, and grasses; birds, bees
and wasps fly around me and even under logs and bushes I find many
surprises. Oh, and do I like looking for them!

I have fun playing by myself because I know that my mother is nearby watching me. However, if I find another porcupette in the woods we play together and we are very happy. We grunt and squeal as we chase each other in circles.

I can swim naturally without needing to be taught how to swim! My tube-like quills have spongy material in them and this airy filling helps me float near the surface of the water. I found this out when my mother and I went to eat plants growing in the water at the pond near our nest.

Climbing trees is not as natural an act as swimming. My mother has to call and coax me to learn to do this. I am very cautious at first, but I soon learn how to grip the bark with my sharp claws. I climb down tail first, and use the stiff brush under it for support.

I must tell you that I am quite safe when I climb a tree. My sharp
curved claws and padded feet are excellent helps for climbing up and
down trees. I can climb almost to the top of high trees. My four toes on
my front feet and my five toes on my hind feet are certainly helpful.

My mother teaches me how to defend myself. One night, I watched a coyote come towards us. My mother sensed the danger and turned her back towards it. She put her head between her front legs, chattered her teeth and arched her back. Thousands of the 30,000 quills that she has stood up on her back and tail. As the coyote reached for my mother, she struck him with her club-like tail which is full of quills. His face was filled with quills! Oh, did he howl and run away!

Coyotes, foxes, owls, and even dogs, are some of our enemies. Wolverines, bears, bobcats, and lynx are even more dangerous. However, the fisher is the most dangerous, and it is my number one enemy.

I leave my mother and begin living by myself when I am between two and three months old.

At that time my quills are their full size. Those around my face are about 1.3 cm (1/2 an inch) long and those on my tail are 7.5 cm (2 and ¾ inches) long. They are loose on my skin and come out easily when I hit my enemy with my tail.

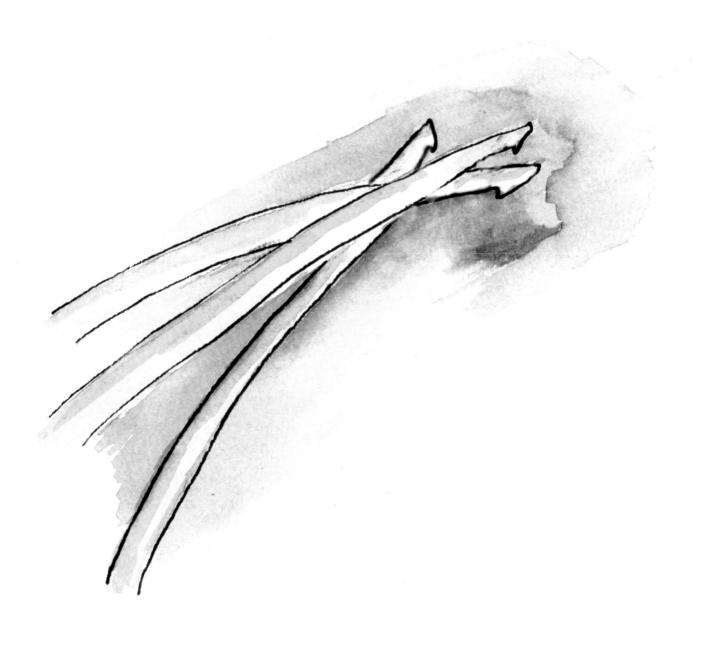

My quills are barbed at the tips. They are like fishhooks and it is very hard to pull them out of the skin because they spread out and hold tight beneath the skin.

I am very slow moving, so I can never outrun my enemies. I don't need to do that! I simply wait until my enemy approaches me; next I erect the thousands of quills on my back and tail, then I strike my enemy with my quill-studded tail.

My dark brown color also protects me. It blends with the dark color of the tree trunks and camouflages me. My enemies can pass by and not even notice me.

When I am not in danger, my quills lie flat beneath an outer coat of guard hairs. These are softer than my quills and these help support the quills when I raise them. My guard hairs also grow longer in winter and help keep me warm.

My four front teeth, called incisors, are very helpful. They are made for cutting and gnawing. They grow throughout my life. Gnawing hard bark helps keep them the right size for my mouth. I have also learned that grinding my teeth against each other while chewing my food does the same thing.

My back teeth are called molars. They are flat and are made for chewing my food. My jaws are also very strong. Because my jaw muscles are so strong, and my incisors very sharp, I am able to eat bark in the wintertime.

I am a vegetarian, or plant-eating animal. Finding food in the spring, summer, and fall is easy. There is plenty of new growth - buds, leaves, grasses, and even new trees. In the autumn there are many berries. Of course, in winter I eat the bark straight off the trees. I do not store food for the winter.

Neither do I sleep the winter away. I am active throughout the winter. I cannot dig so I always find ready-made dens - old tree stumps, hollow trees, caves, and abandoned dens or rock piles. When it's really cold I can stay in my den for days.

When I am three years old, I will find a mate and we will have a new porcupette together. I will live and grow quietly in the woods. Under normal conditions I can live to be fifteen years old.

The word porcupine comes from the French words "porc", which means pig, and "epine", which means spine. Spine is also another word for thorn, or quill. That is why porcupines are also called "quill pigs". Why pigs? Because people think that our snorting noises make us sound like pigs and our large nostrils make us look like pigs.